Dr. Cliff's Notes
on
A SIMPLE STUDYING METHOD THAT WORKS

Cliff C. Morris Jr., PhD

Copyright © 2018 Cliff C. Morris, Jr. PhD
ISBN 978-0-9971980-8-9

All Rights Reserved.

No part of this book may be reproduced or transmitted in any form or by any means, electronically or mechanically, including photocopying, recording or by an information storage and retrieval system without permission in writing from the author of this book.

Interior & Cover Layout & Design:
Tarsha L. Campbell

Published by:
DOMINIONHOUSE
Publishing & Design, LLC
P.O. Box 681938 | Orlando, Florida 32868 | 407.703.4800
www.mydominionhouse.com

Acknowledgment

I would like to gratefully acknowledge my wife, Angela Reed Morris, my children now grown and raising their own children, our grandchildren, and the Lord Jesus, the Messiah who has inspired much of my work. I also would like to gratefully acknowledge the many students who have contributed to the development of this book.

"...If one expects a different set of outcomes, they must do something or some things they have never done."

Table of Contents

Foreword 7

First Things First – Assembling the Tools 13

Next – The Method 17

Continuing the Method and Moving Forward. . 23

Let's Review the Method Thus Far. 33

A Final Part of Our Method that Delivers
More for the Student........................ 39

Final Comments, Final Encouragements...... 49

About the Author 52

"I have shared this method I am writing about here with students and have seen their results go through the roof. Some have come back to tell me they surpassed their previous expectations and were genuinely grateful because I shared these study principles with them."

FOREWORD

I have encountered over my forty plus years of teaching mathematics both at the high school and collegiate level many students who have had an inadequate idea of what studying actually is or what studying entails. I have heard many of these students declare that doing or completing homework is, in their mind, studying. They actually complete their assignments only to find they are woefully lacking in understanding of the essential material they claim to have studied, and worse, they fail to understand why their grades continue to spiral downward after they have done their homework and, in their minds, studied. Many of our students have spent hours studying right before a major examination and many times in a marathon overnight effort only to find the outcome did not justify the labor, if one can call this studying.

DR. CLIFF'S NOTES:
A SIMPLE STUDYING METHOD THAT WORKS

We have heard of stories of students who slough off for much of the semester, losing precious time, and decide to cram at the last minute in hopes of delivering high, or at least decent, scores on examinations when the amount of material has grown beyond their abilities to master in a single evening or two prior to this major examination.

After hearing this banter from my students and other instructor's students over the years, I have come to the conclusion that their lack of comprehension of this important student behavior is tragic and that they are in need of substantive assistance from those of us who have enjoyed much richer success in accomplishing the art of studying.

It turns out a few modifications together with an understanding of how our minds work will deliver powerful understanding and mastery of any course material. I say this because I was then and am currently a professor of mathematics. In fact, I was dean of the Department of Mathematics at Valencia College for fourteen of the thirty years I was employed there.

FOREWORD

I have shared this method I am writing about here with students and have seen their results go through the roof. Some have come back to tell me they surpassed their previous expectations and were genuinely grateful because I shared these study principles with them. Just recently, I shared this study method with two students at a university in the Central Florida area. After sharing this method, I checked in with both the students by mobile phone periodically to see how they were faring. Follow-up can be very helpful to ensure the parties are completing their assignments after learning a new method. While the young man involved did not continue with this method (I'm not sure how his grades turned out), the young lady earned her first four-point average that semester. Yes, she earned all A's in all credit courses at her university and was delighted after not faring so well in previous semesters. I need not tell you her parents were pleasantly surprised, particularly since her weakest subject was her statistics class.

DR. CLIFF'S NOTES:
A SIMPLE STUDYING METHOD THAT WORKS

Insanity, it is said, is doing the same thing over and over, expecting different results. If one desires the same results, they need to only continue to do what they have always done. If one desires a different set of outcomes, they must do something or some things they have never done.

Studying involves the student's behavior after he or she has completed their homework. In the remainder of this book, I will outline how to set up your study routine, outline the learning strategies behind it, and get you moving onward toward a successful and somewhat enjoyable learning experience that pays superior dividends.

This method does involve spending some money. But you will find that you can prepare for and use this method with less than $5 per course for the entire semester. I hope you will see how powerful this set of exercises is and that you will enjoy the ride while you are preparing to perform the best you have ever performed in your elementary, high school, college, or graduate career.

FOREWORD

I developed this method while in graduate school at the University of South Florida in Tampa, Florida. Though I have heard bits and pieces of various study methods across the years from others, I have fashioned my own version and am now writing about it and its ability to deliver positive results for and to you. Be encouraged! We are about to turn the tables on bad habits and bad thinking. Stay with me.

"Making strong, positive grades will open new vistas for you, bring you into the company of great people, and prepare you for a successful world with support right through the graduate degree of your choice with someone else, not you, footing the total cost."

CHAPTER 1

FIRST THINGS FIRST – ASSEMBLING THE TOOLS

We will need to purchase one of the main tools for this study routine. I would like for you to go to any Dollar General, Dollar Tree, Family Dollar, or similar retail outlet and buy a set of index cards, preferably a set of 100 cards. There are generally three sizes available. They are of the 3x5, 4x6, or 5x8 variety. I generally suggest buying the 4x6 cards. I will explain later why this is preferable. This set of 100 cards will cost about one dollar unless inflation has inched the price up. They will do fine for us and present the best opportunity for us to engage this system of study.

What I am about to describe is simple to do but will cost you time and effort to assemble

DR. CLIFF'S NOTES:
A SIMPLE STUDYING METHOD THAT WORKS

the set of tools that will push you down the road of understanding and cogency. Why index cards?

The cards are portable, a definite need you will enjoy after a few weeks of working with these cards. I will seek to separate you from your cumbersome notebook with all your notes and from your textbook as well. I will describe how even though your textbook and notebook are important in and of themselves, it is really what is in both your textbook and notebook that are vital. You will be shown how to highlight the most important information in both your textbook and notebook and use your portable study minions, the index cards, to shape your own portable combination of these instruments. I prefer the 4x6 card size because these cards are larger than the 3x5 cards but remain portable for placement in your shirt pocket or casual purse.

I trust you are ready now to really take control of your studying and get busy making great grades in your classes. Making strong, positive

FIRST THINGS FIRST – ASSEMBLING THE TOOLS

grades will open new vistas for you, bring you into the company of great people, and prepare you for a successful world with support right through the graduate degree of your choice with someone else, not you, footing the total cost. This can happen for you. Let's get started.

" The instructors tend to drop hints as to the kind of problem or problems they enjoy quizzing you on. Do not ignore these hints being dropped. Instructors will also let you know when you may not expect a certain type of problem on a text. Do not ignore that hint either."

CHAPTER 2

NEXT – THE METHOD

You now have purchased the first set of 100 or so index cards of the size you desire from your local dollar retail store. How will these cards be used? Let's assume you are in an algebra course. This would be easier for me to explain since I taught algebra for over 40 years. However, you may apply the same techniques I will explain to any other secondary or collegiate subject.

After your first lesson in algebra, the instructor will generally assign homework. This is where you begin this method of arranging your system of study.

After completing your homework (important), take a few minutes to look over your completed assignment.

DR. CLIFF'S NOTES:
A SIMPLE STUDYING METHOD THAT WORKS

You want to select between five and seven problems from the completed assignment and reduce each selected problem to an index card in a particular fashion as follows below. Select maybe one or two problems that may be simple (from the first few examples assigned). Select the remaining examples not from the more difficult problems generally at the end of the assigned exercises but from those nearest the middle of the exercises. The exception would be if the instructor seemed to favor a more difficult problem. Then you would want to select at least one in this range of the material.

Here is an example of exactly how you want to make your first card. This pattern will be used for all index cards you will create. Let us suppose you are studying solving linear equations containing a single variable. The assignment will have a question stem followed by a problem you will need to solve.

You are going to write the question stem on the front of the index card. On the back of the

NEXT – THE METHOD

card, you will actually work out the problem in detail and write any notes you need to foster comprehension of that problem (cheat notes that are actually helpful suggestions to remember anything you may forget otherwise).

EXAMPLE: 5. Solve for x. $3x + 5 = 11$

On the front of the index card, you will actually write out the question stem shown above. The question stem then is . . .

---
5. Solve for x. $3x + 5 = 11$

On the back of the card, you will actually solve the equation for x as shown below.

> $3x + 5 = 11$
> $-5 -5$
> (add – 5 to both sides to separate the variables)
> ----------------
> $3x = 6$ (+5–5=0 left, 11–5=6 right)
> $3x/3 = 6/3$ (divide both sides by 3 to solve for x)
> $x = 2$ (answer)

> Check: $3(2) + 5 = 11$, Yes, this checks! (You do not have to write this but it may help to check.)

What you have seen is how to construct your first index card for one of five to seven cards for this unit on solving linear equations that contain a single variable. Note I am using mathematical language to describe what I am doing. This is important in learning mathematics – to know how to express what you are working out in words.

You are now prepared to continue to make the additional cards (four to six additional cards for this set of exercises assigned by your instructor).

NEXT – THE METHOD

Let us now assume you have completed your five to seven index cards. This means you have isolated the five to seven assigned problems first (not the easiest and not the most difficult . . . middle of the road problems most likely to be asked on a test). You should know here that most instructors rarely depart from the kinds of problems they ask on examinations from term to term. Instructors tend to drop hints as to the kind of problem or problems they enjoy quizzing you on. Do not ignore these hints being dropped. Instructors will also let you know when you may not expect a certain type of problem on a text. Do not ignore that hint either. Pay attention to the type of problems they put on quizzes as these types are strongly suggestive of examples you might expect on the chapter/unit tests.

" It is relatively well known from learning research that the brain is able to retain comfortably what is presented in the first ten minutes and the last ten minutes of study time. This should cause some concern as some of our learning institutions seem at times to be completely unaware of this phenomenon."

CHAPTER 3

CONTINUING THE METHOD AND MOVING FORWARD

Let us assume you are now armed with one set of index cards with problems from that first problem set. You may also imagine that eventually you have completed three sets of five to seven examples in the manner I have outlined (question stem on a single side, probably the ruled side, and the problem actually worked out completely on the flip side with any notes you wish to add). This procedure I am suggesting now will be used throughout the remainder of the course.

Another feature of this study technique is that you will carry these cards with you almost everywhere you go. I am suggesting you will be taking the WHOLE set of cards with you either in your shirt pocket or in some holster linked to your belt or in your purse or backpack. I would suggest you use a rubber band or card case to transport these instruments with you in an orderly fashion. This is very important for the reasons I am about to share with you.

It is relatively well known from learning research that the brain is able to retain comfortably what is presented in the first ten minutes and the last ten minutes of study time. This should cause some concern as some of our learning institutions seem at times to be completely unaware of this phenomenon. Our secondary schools and our collegiate institutions hold lessons ranging in duration from 50 minutes per class to almost three hours, if not longer in some cases. We have an opportunity to shape our acquisition of this material by tailoring our study habits to take advantage of what we know from the research on learning.

What does this then say about studying or cramming six hours prior to an examination? It appears we are really wasting five hours and forty minutes on this marathon learning expedition. The public court is still out on whether

CONTINUING THE METHOD AND MOVING FORWARD

this method of last minute studying has a globally positive outcome for the many students resorting to this exercise. I propose the following.

You assume a comfortable position in a seat and use your set of index cards as you would a set of flash cards. Place each card in front of you for a few seconds or more at first. Read the question stem, then try to see how to mentally resolve or work this problem in your mind. After a few seconds, turn the card over and read through the steps to solve this problem (make additional notes if needed to aid in remembering how and what to do to solve your problem).

This next point is VITALLY IMPORTANT!!! You must use these cards for twenty minutes only at a time! Then take OFF (put the cards down) twenty minutes or half hour if you choose. Then go back and use the cards again, twenty minutes on the cards, then <u>twenty to thirty minutes OFF the cards</u>.

DR. CLIFF'S NOTES:
A SIMPLE STUDYING METHOD THAT WORKS

You should see this makes complete sense. Many students end up many times not studying because they put themselves in a position to NOT study. How many times have you promised to study two to three hours only to find yourself ending up not studying because that chunk of time is unavailable or you get busy and forget to study?

Twenty minutes (a shorter interval of time) is so much easier to handle. People have twenty minutes all day, every day. They generally will find this smaller time interval manageable.

I have never gone into a barber shop and immediately gotten into a chair to get my haircut. While waiting for an open chair, I will take out my index cards from my shirt or coat pocket and do twenty minutes on, twenty minutes off until my turn comes. If I am in a traffic jam, I will take out my cards and get five to ten minutes while waiting for the jam to loosen up. It also keeps me from boiling over in anger because I am not in control of the traffic. Try this for yourself.

CONTINUING THE METHOD
AND MOVING FORWARD

The same is true for our lady friends. They don't get immediately into a chair at the hair salon even with an appointment, right? They can remove their index cards from their purses or pocket books and get their twenty minutes on, twenty minutes off while waiting for their hair appointment or pedicure, or manicure, or massage.

I recommend you work on formulas needing memorization with the index cards. For example, you may need to actually know the quadratic formula for an upcoming examination. I would suggest you set this up on an index card as follows.

Front of index card:

State the quadratic formula

Back of index card:

$$x = \frac{-b \pm \sqrt{b^2 - 4ac}}{2a}$$

DR. CLIFF'S NOTES:
A SIMPLE STUDYING METHOD THAT WORKS

You would then approach the index card on the front side and try to state this formula from memory. After a few seconds, turn over the card to the back and check to see how good you have become until you have mastered this memorization.

Remember, if you have covered five chapters with six sections in each chapter, you should now have with you thirty sets of index cards. This means you have from 150 to 210 index cards available for you to complete your twenty minutes on, twenty minutes off until the course is over.

Notice that you have stripped the most important information from both your text and in-class notes to formulate or boil down for test prep acquisition. And all your homework is done. You can feel proud of using this method to almost effortlessly imbibe the critical information that will lead to a successful test-taking strategy.

CONTINUING THE METHOD
AND MOVING FORWARD

You have also gained another advantage because you have tailored your study to smaller chunks of information while using smaller chunks of time mastering this material. You will tend to feel more relaxed and confident in your studying over time instead of dreading the hour-upon-hour marathon you would normally feel obliged to engage in because you have not taken the time to study for some weeks now.

From time to time, you may want to leave some of the earlier sets of index cards at home or at your dormitory. This will probably be fine since you will know after several weeks where you are in the class and hopefully feel confident that some of the material is frozen in your memory where you will not need some of the cards. Guys and gals, the twenty minutes on, twenty minutes off works.

I kind of hate to confess this, but I actually studied while watching some of my favorite shows on TV during some evenings. The commercials tend to be long, sometimes several minutes. With the remote in hand, I would mute the TV during the commercial and get in 7-10 minutes of studying while the commercials were on. My kids would see me using my flash cards, looking at the cards, then putting them down, then turning the cards over to check my thinking and answers. Both are important. I must get the sequential thinking working for me. Afterwards, the correct answer should present itself. Learning was taking place even in front of the TV. Please don't tell anyone this. This is between you and me.

CONTINUING THE METHOD AND MOVING FORWARD

Use the space below for notes.

> By studying as suggested, you are establishing mental, not written, connections with the material. We know from research that students remember the first ten minutes and the last ten minutes of what they have studied."

CHAPTER 4

LET'S REVIEW THE METHOD THUS FAR

To gain the advantage in studying as shown previously, we need to embrace the following.

1. Purchase an initial set or two of 100 index cards (ruled or unruled) from the dollar store. As mentioned previously, these sets of index cards give you portability. We are able to study anywhere and in many types of settings (barber shop, city park, college campus, Wendy's, the mall, even at our places of employment). We do not have to be burdened down with our textbooks or notebooks, just a set of cards we carry either in our purses, pocketbooks, or shirt/coat pockets. You will have distilled all the important information onto your cards, freeing you from lugging all your books and notebooks for your classes.

DR. CLIFF'S NOTES:
A SIMPLE STUDYING METHOD THAT WORKS

2. On our very first assignment or exercise, you will identify between 5 and 7 examples that are easy to medium difficulty. You then make an index card for each problem, writing the question stem on the front side of the card, then the completely worked out example on the back of the card (with additional notes if necessary). You continue this for any and all sets of assignments provided by the instructor. After five sets of exercises assigned, you should end up with 25 to 35 index cards to study with.

3. You now begin what has been previously set up, twenty minutes on studying, twenty minutes off studying. By studying as suggested, you are establishing mental, not written, connections with the material. We know from research that students remember the first ten minutes and the last ten minutes of what they have studied. You are using this research result to compose this twenty minutes on, twenty minutes off (rest) routine.

LET'S REVIEW THE METHOD THUS FAR

The off part of this method provides the needed breaks from studying, permitting the brain to reset after imbibing the material. I have over the years observed many students writing nervously without cultivating the mental flow of the examples. This appears to be a hallmark of western study habits. The students are confused when a slightly different problem appears on the examination. The method suggested takes the pencil or pen away from the students so they may focus on the mental derivations and connections with the examples to obtain a more suitable and lasting result. The students are also more able to see developmental connections among the sequential problem sets and see how later concepts build on what was previously learned. This is highly important in learning mathematics. I would think this is also highly important in learning in any discipline.

4. I would lastly suggest the student consider arranging the index cards out of order from time to time in an effort to determine how strong his/her retention of the whole of the material is. This would be helpful in an effort to prepare for the final examination that is a breadth examination (whole range of material where there is more material and less depth) rather than a depth examination (covering a single chapter or unit where there is less material and more depth).

LET'S REVIEW THE METHOD THUS FAR

Use the space below for notes.

> There is much to learn through this method. You will for the first time know what you know, and more importantly, what you are missing from the topics covered by this test. Once this test has been scored or graded, use the graded test to add the topics needing attention to your index cards."

CHAPTER 5

A FINAL PART OF OUR METHOD THAT DELIVERS MORE FOR THE STUDENT
(Optional, but recommended)

A final suggestion regarding this method of studying involves direct test preparation. It is in this portion of study that great gains can be made. These gains will show up in a better attitude and expected outcomes for the student, better management of time during the test, and stronger self-confidence. These ingredients will make a better, more able student while delivering stronger grades in the course. If handled efficiently, the student will not only become more self-confident and deliver better grades but the improved performance will launch a stronger appreciation for learning since success will breed continued success. This portion of this set of study techniques alone can make the student competitive for additional aid in grants, scholarships, and various other awards of credit that can, and I believe, will provide a much more stable and lasting educational career with many accolades for the student. Of course, my best wishes go with you. You can do it! Now, on to describe this final method of study.

I mentioned earlier that many instructors tend to favor a set of problems for every test, in every course they teach, and across multiple semesters. These instructors have a database of examinations they tend to use over and over again. Depending on the instructor, they may actually use the exact same examinations from grading period to grading period. Other instructors may vary the numbers in their examples without changing much else from grading period to grading period. Still others will actually re-engineer a new test each time and perhaps, just perhaps, use a previous test as a guide in structuring the newest version of a chapter or midterm or final examination. This last option was actually what I preferred to use from semester to semester while I was teaching mathematics at the collegiate level. Here is what I suggest you do to utilize what I have just shared.

A FINAL PART OF OUR METHOD THAT DELIVERS MORE FOR THE STUDENT

Make an appointment to speak with your instructor in their office or at school at least a week before each chapter/unit test. The purpose of this visit is to ask your instructor for a copy of a sample test prior to each unit test. Try to obtain two different sample tests if they have additional copies or will allow this. This will mean that if your instructor typically gives five tests in a regular semester, you will end up with ten practice tests if the instructor will permit you to obtain these copies. To be clear, you will not ask for all ten copies at one time. You will make separate appointments with the idea of asking for one or two copies of the upcoming chapter/unit examination. Now, armed with the copy(ies), you will do the following.

Set aside the same amount of time that the test is to be administered. For example, if your test will last for fifty (50) minutes in the classroom, set aside that precise amount of time for your mock test. Use the timer on your watch or purchase an inexpensive timer to give a beep when this testing time is over.

DR. CLIFF'S NOTES:
A SIMPLE STUDYING METHOD THAT WORKS

Of course, you may observe the timer as you are completing this test.

No theater expecting to present a play to the public does so without a dress rehearsal. The actors must do more than just quote lines, hone various gestures, and make sweeping movements that show mastery of relationships between people and spaces on stage. They need to combine all of their acting skills and talents in full dress. This is highly important! Otherwise, surprises will occur that can damage and obliterate all of the talents and skills the actors have worked so hard to perfect for their collective performances. Anyone in theater or motion pictures or school plays knows how vastly important this dress rehearsal is. I am suggesting we create a dress rehearsal for our upcoming examination. This will strongly address many issues students face while in school.

I have counseled students who admitted that they have test anxiety. After much studying, they tell me they just lose it on the test.

A FINAL PART OF OUR METHOD THAT DELIVERS MORE FOR THE STUDENT

I have found this phenomenon to be true. Students do experience test-taking anxiety. This anxiety shows up in the literature all the time with many suggestions for how to minimize it, if not completely cure the student. What I am proposing now is a way of at least minimizing this anxiety.

After securing a copy of a sample test from your instructor, you want to set aside the same amount of time as for the examination. Make sure you have your test-taking tools (scratch paper, pen or pencil, calculator if one is required, etc.). Set your timer (watch or actual timer) first. Set your test and your tools on a table or desk if possible.

Set your time, fill out your sample test with your name and the date if needed and begin to take this test in the time allotted. Do your best. If you encounter a problem that you do not know how to begin, try skipping this question and move on to the next one.

DR. CLIFF'S NOTES:
A SIMPLE STUDYING METHOD THAT WORKS

Do not spend too much time on any problem you do not recognize. Move on. Come back to that question later. Complete the examination taking as much time as is left in the alloted time to finish problems you were unsure about. If you finish the test before the time allotted, please go back and check your answers. You should be able to remember much from your index cards since you have been mentally connecting with the material during your study time.

Once you have completed the test and the time has been expended, I would suggest you get this test graded by a competent student or mathematics instructor. There is much to learn via this method. You will for the first time know what you know, and more importantly, what you are missing from the topics covered by this test. Once this test has been scored or graded, use the graded test to add the topics needing attention to your index cards. Match the topics to the cards where this material was being taught or displayed. You now have the opportunity to strengthen this material

A FINAL PART OF OUR METHOD THAT DELIVERS MORE FOR THE STUDENT

by mentally going over this work. Many students do not think of taking a sample test as a part of their study routine. They tend to think the brighter students have all the advantages, so what's the use? The smarter students, as you say, may have a more superior studying routine than you. They are not much smarter than you. They study smarter, not harder. You can do this.

I suggest you use the second test to do exactly what you did for the first test. The advantage now is that you have some information about where your weaknesses are and a chance to capitalize on developing strategies to strengthen those weaknesses.

If you are wondering about the time frame for this particular part of your study routine, I have a suggestion. You want to take the first sample test under the actual time constraints no less than two days before the test is scheduled. If you can arrange the mock test three days before, this might work out better for you. This way, you can have the test graded and go through the results to see what you have mastered and especially what needs some more work (twenty minutes on, twenty minutes off).

After this first sample test has been graded and you have completed your follow-up work in strengthening the topics not yet mastered, take the second sample test under the same time constraints you observed on the first sample test. If you are unable to obtain a second sample test, taking that first one is incredibly important. Do not stress if a second sample test is unavailable. You should fare much better if you have at least a single shot at a sample test.

If for some reason, you are unable to secure any sample test from the instructor, you may be able to obtain a copy from a former student of that particular instructor. This is one of the reasons fraternities and sororities exist. They have files and files of tests and worksheets of professors on campus that are available for those

A FINAL PART OF OUR METHOD THAT DELIVERS MORE FOR THE STUDENT

who are members of that fraternity or sorority. If you are friends with these folks, please feel free to ask them for a copy of a former test to use for your dress rehearsal.

Finally, make sure you get in a full eight hours of restful sleep the night before the official testing date. This rest will have a great favorable impact on test readiness, reduce anxiety, and is supported by learning research as well. When coming into the testing room, do not engage in banter with your classmates about what you studied and did not study. This kind of comparative chat will have the effect of producing unwanted test anxiety and can undo your advantage. Remember, you have been preparing for this test very differently than many others in the class. This preparation will provide the edge in your favor. Speak politely. Afterwards, get to your desk, assemble your testing tools, and prepare to do well without the typical distractions of anxiety-filled conversations. You can do this! We are counting on you!

> During that time, I have had the rare opportunity to observed students' lives change before my eyes. I have witnessed them unsure of themselves at first. As the semester progresses, they become more comfortable as they become aware that they are able to not only learn the material being presented but that they become masters of that material."

CHAPTER 6

FINAL COMMENTS, FINAL ENCOURAGEMENTS

I have very much enjoyed sharing these studying trade secrets with you, our students.

A wise man once stated, "If you find a job you love, you will never work the rest of your life." I really believe and have been the embodiment of that epitaph. I have taught students for over forty years and have enjoyed every moment I have been in the classroom. During that time, I have had the rare opportunity to observe students' lives change before my eyes. I have witnessed them unsure of themselves at first. As the semester progresses, they become more comfortable as they become aware that they are able to not only learn the material being presented but that they become masters of that material. The light in their eyes highlights the wonderful story of discovery and worth as a student and person.

DR. CLIFF'S NOTES:
A SIMPLE STUDYING METHOD THAT WORKS

You who are reading this material can feel free to contact me, Dr. Cliff Morris, Jr. at any time. My email address is clissle@me.com. You may also contact me via the worldwide web at http://www.cliff.guru. You may also contact me at 407-963-MATH (that's 407-963-6284 for those of you who prefer the digits). Enjoy your days on this earth. We can and should brighten the days of and for our students. Peace.

FINAL COMMENTS, FINAL ENCOURAGEMENTS

Use the space below for notes.

────────── About the Author ──────────

Dr. Cliff C. Morris, Jr. is a native of Fort Pierce, Florida, where he graduated second in his class from Lincoln Park Academy in 1969. He attended the Florida Agricultural and Mechanical University (FAMU) where he majored in mathematics and graduated in 1973. After teaching high school for a year, he entered and completed a master's program in mathematics education.

He was hired by the Central Florida Community College CETA Program, where he spent about a month serving until he was chosen to teach mathematics at Valencia Community College. He completed a thirty-year tenure there and retired as Dean of the Department of Mathematics.

His other interests included leading the Tribes of EL Bethel Temple of Jesus International, where he is the Senior Bishop/CEO. He inherited this position from the former Senior Bishop Archie Williams, Sr.

Dr. Morris loves helping people of all cultures and has traveled six of the seven continents of the world spreading his love for serving. He has volunteered for VOSH (Volunteer Optometric Services for Humanity), has taught mathematics in Cape Town, South Africa, and continues to do so semi-annually each year.

This small publishing project has grown out of his desire for students to develop a routine for studying that will enhance and better organize their academic lives. As he has found this information helpful for students he has encountered while teaching, he hopes this project finds its mark in assisting future students and those he may not have a chance to personally engage.

He is married to Angela Reed Morris and they collectively have eight grown children and thirteen grandchildren.

www.ingramcontent.com/pod-product-compliance
Lightning Source LLC
Chambersburg PA
CBHW050448010526
44118CB00013B/1732